What if the Problem's
Not the
Problem???

4 Practices for
Peace of Mind

Jasmyne Boswell

Preface by Peter Fenner, Ph.D.
Author of *Radiant Mind* and *Reasoning into Reality*

ISBN: 1467950521
ISBN 13: 9781467950527

Library of Congress Control Number: 2012905408
Createspace, North Charleston, SC

To my son Robert James Boswell

Acknowledgments

While writing this book, I'm aware of how lucky I am to have heard a call that beckoned me to follow the path of Self-discovery. I am in continual, deep gratitude for all beings whether in the form of human, animal or plant life who share their enlightened perspectives. To that which cannot be known, thank you for all your blessings and for the consciousness that allows us to enjoy the fruits of creation.

I give a special thanks to Peter Fenner, Ph.D. He and his Radiant Mind course (RM) were my muses as I wrote this book. I am ever so appreciative for the profoundly simply practices his course offered that pointed me toward a peaceful way of being. I am also immensely grateful for the conscious community of men and women in Boulder, Colorado and beyond, with whom I shared the four-year RM journey. Their love, vulnerability and humility opened my heart and mind and made those four years unforgettable.

To my Hawaii sisters, Beth Marcil and Helen Kritzler, who enthusiastically asked to read my finished draft and gave me valuable, insightful feedback, Mahalo nui loa and ho`omaika`I (many thanks and appreciation). Mahalo to my dear friends, Margo and John Steiner, who read and helped me refine my final draft. I am deeply touched by your generosity of spirit.

And, Mahalo, Mahalo to my writing students, family and friends who listened to my earliest rough drafts. Your interest was inspiring and kept me going.

Contents

Preface

Jasmyne Boswell is a delightful, exuberant and wise woman. I first met her as a participant in a Radiant Mind course. She went on to do this course three times and also completed an Advanced Nondual Training. She threw herself into these trainings wholeheartedly with a verve and vigor that was inspiring for other participants. There were four particular practices within Radiant Mind that touched her deeply. She took them and worked with them thoroughly throughout the course and beyond. This often happens. Three or four practices out of the twenty or so that are presented in Radiant Mind jump out at someone. They speak to their heart and take root as living koans. People apply them across the board, in every area of their lives.

In this book Jasmyne draws on her life experience—as a seeker, mother, lover and business woman—and shows us how to bring a real and stable level of fulfillment to our lives. She shares with us a different quality of being that comes alive when we leave our old patterns of blame and fear behind us and encounter life with a new found courage that arises when we live in and for the present moment.

Jasmyne shows us how our problems are *not* what we usually think they are. What we say is the problem—our relationships, our financial situation, even our health—isn't, fundamentally, the problem. The problem is that we make our circumstances into a problem. Jasmyne shows us how nothing is problematic in the instant it is arising. Every moment takes care of itself.

We are introduced to a new way of listening to ourselves: a way of listening that reveals a subtle, steady voice deep within that serves as a reliable source of guidance and direction. This way of listening pierces through the chatter of our superficial thoughts and brings to light the subtle messages that connect with the totality of our being, and which point to a more wholesome way of living. As you read this book, you will learn how to be complete in each and every moment, and how to regularly access a state of natural meditation.

I'm confident that you will benefit from her inspired words. If you take the practices she describes and outlines to heart, you'll discover a new life—a life that's less restrained and more spontaneous, yet which is also rooted in, and guided by, the intelligence of inner wisdom. I suspect that within just a few weeks of working with the inquiries and exercises that Jasmyne includes at the end of each chapter you'll be listening with confidence from a space deep within you that is depthless, immutable, peace itself, and which will show you how to encounter your life with a new found capacity for self-less contribution and daring creativity.

I trust that you will enjoy this inspiring book.

Warm wishes,
Peter Fenner, Ph.D.
Creator of Radiant Mind and
Natural Awakening
www.nondualtraining.com

Introduction

If peace of mind is what you're after, this book may be just what you're looking for. It will give you the simple truth about what it takes to feel at peace in your everyday experience.

In 2005 I wasn't actively looking for my life to change—not that much anyway. But I did have that feeling, "Is this all there is?" It had been a couple of years since I'd been in a real relationship. My marketing business was coasting along but not giving me the juice or the income I'd been used to. I loved having my eldest son close by and sharing in his life, but a lot of my close friends had moved from Boulder, Colorado where I was living, and I was missing the deep intimacy that had provided. No one would have guessed I was feeling empty. I was getting along "just fine." All I really wanted was something to stir things up a bit.

As luck would have it, a friend of mine called and told me to check out the teachings of Peter Fenner, Ph.D. He said Peter was coming to Boulder to give an introductory talk for his upcoming Radiant Mind Training. I checked out his website and was intrigued. At the talk I immediately felt drawn to his experiential style of teaching. I also knew many of the people signing up for his upcoming course. Loving conscious community, I climbed on board.

During the four years I stayed with the training, I questioned my beliefs with serious focus and thankfully, lots of laughter. I astounded myself as I saw how entangled I was in survival techniques that kept me safe from judgment— my own as well as others. During the weekend intensives, one by one, my beliefs popped into view and I'd feel the stranglehold they had on me. Not brand new to growth work I was able to laugh and ask myself, "What the hell were you thinking?" Everyone in the group seemed to be going through a similar process. When we delved into discovery together, we cracked each other up. Especially when we witnessed our minds grasping to understand every nuance of every detail that we soon realized had little or no relevance. *Nothing was sacred*.

Many valuable teachings were offered during the course, but there were four particular practices I worked with that greatly enhanced all the teachings I'd experienced to date. These four practices changed my life. By integrating them into daily living, all the stress and struggle previously experienced miraculously melted away and I was at peace.

Most of us desire peace of mind even if just for moments at a time. And yet in a world that is constantly changing, it gets harder to depend on anything external to meet this deep longing. Finding ways to address the challenges to our emotional, physical and spiritual health has become a necessity.

In this book I offer you the four practices that brought me a sense of well-being that doesn't waver no matter what the outer circumstances look like.

The four practices are: *1) What if your Problem's not the Problem?* Putting an end to resistance. 2) *Doing what's Obvious:* honoring the natural flow of life. 3) *Being Complete in the Moment:* finding peace in the middle of any storm: 4) *Pure Awareness***:** residing in our natural state of being.

As a result of working with these practices, I've learned to enjoy the sense of peace, calm and spaciousness that rests in each moment. It's as if I took an iron to my nervous system and smoothed out the wrinkles.

To make the information easy to assimilate the entries include relatable stories, inquiries, key pointers and exercises. The material can be applied to everyday challenges, both big and small, including relationship frustrations, losing a job, raising children and even the death of a loved one. They are profoundly simple and make living in today's chaotic world uncomplicated and effortless.

Once I recognized the subtleties that deterred me from this ease, and those that led me toward it, I changed my relationship with life. From there, the magic and grace available became more vivid.

Learning to enjoy this peace and everything life presents, continues to be my holy grail. And like everything that's good in life, it begs to be shared. I offer you this book with love.

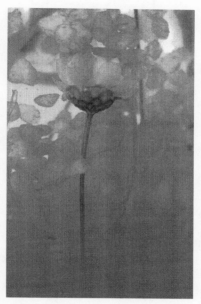

"We have rudiments of reverence for the human body, but we consider as nothing the rape of the human mind."
~Eric Hoffer

I

Changing Perspective

A contemporary fable, The Wizard of Oz, brilliantly portrays the pull the thinking mind has on the psyche. It captivates Dorothy and her friends who believe their thoughts (dreams) to be real until . . . . . The Good Witch of the North, Dorothy's wise intuitive self, tells her to click the heels of her magic, red shoes and voilà, she's home.

There's really no way to escape our innate brilliance, but we might have to change our perspective to experience it.

I was a mother of two small boys when I was awakened from my personal fairy tale. My pictures of the perfect house, with the perfect husband and the two perfect children evaporated the night I confronted my husband about having an affair and he confirmed my nightmare. I was devastated. I left him not knowing if it would be forever, but at least for now I was a mother of two small boys in the process of separating from a seven-year marriage.

Settling into my new life, I soon realized that adjusting to the breakup of my family was only half of the transition I faced. Although I was 26 years old chronologically, I felt as if I were only 19 in experience and found myself where I'd left off when I married and exited the dating scene. At first I felt like a kid in a candy store with no adult around to monitor her appetite. I soon found a girlfriend, also a divorcee, who'd been single for a few years. She took me under her wing, taking me to singles clubs and fixing me up with all her ex-boyfriends. For a while the attention I got seemed to piece together my shattered ego and party-down became my middle name.

Then I met John who was different than any of the men I'd met so far. He was more interested in getting to know me than doing recreational drugs and ravishing my sinuous body. Seeing how vulnerable I was, instead of taking advantage of my naïveté, he gave me the name and telephone number of his therapist and said, "I think you'll like Marty and get a lot out of seeing him." John was without a doubt an angel and Marty became my saving grace.

I made the call and an appointment to see Marty the following week. He was just what I needed. Each week I'd arrive at his office and tell him how I was feeling. I'd reiterate the same stories with slightly different headlines about managing my new life and my indecisions about my faltering marriage. Although my ex-husband and I were leading separate lives, occasionally we'd talk about getting back together. I felt confused and wondered, *could I ever trust him again? It would be so much easier on the boys.* I vacillated daily even as I started to enjoy my new found freedom.

After a few sessions, I think Marty was getting just as bored of hearing the same ol' same ol' as I was. In fact, one time I think he actually started to nod off. I sincerely wanted my life to change but didn't know how to make that happen.

Finally, during one session he asked, "Are you willing to play a game with me?"

Trusting him I said, "Sure."

"Then stand up and look at the wall in front of you."

I stood up and looked.

"Really take it in," he continued. "Notice what you see, how you feel, what you think and allow yourself to become completely immersed in that view."

The wall was lined with floor to ceiling bookshelves housing a library of reference books. They looked old. Marty had to be in his 50's. He was balding, at least six feet tall and somewhat overweight. He too seemed old. After a few minutes passed, he said, "Now turn 90 degrees clockwise, look at the adjacent wall and in the same way, take it in."

The second wall was painted white and had a brown wooden door that I assumed was a closet. There was also a green, overstuffed chair in the corner with a framed painting of a city hanging above it. After taking in that wall, I sat back down.

Marty then asked, "When you turned to look at the wall with the green chair, were you still focusing on or thinking about the wall with the bookshelves?"

"No."

"Why not?"

"Because I wasn't looking in that direction," I replied pointing toward the books.

"Would you say you had a different perspective of the room each time you changed direction?"

"Yeah."

"Did you feel differently?" I thought for a moment and nodded wondering where he was going with this.

"Well that's all you have to do to change your life—get a different perspective. Turn your attention away from the traps of your mind *(stop thinking Oz has all the answers)*. Open your eyes and your mind by changing your perspective and see what else life has to offer. From there, you and everything around you will start to change."

It seemed too easy, but what he said penetrated my uncertainty. I experienced a mind-stopping silence I'd grow familiar with as I continued a path of waking up to possibilities beyond my current point of view.

The more conscious I became of my narrow perspectives the more I saw how they limited my experience of life. I'd been living in a self-constructed cage and forgot I could step out any time I wanted to. The more I examined my life, the more I had to let go of what I believed to be true.

Through many years of taking in a multitude of personal and spiritual growth teachings, I became cognizant of the thought patterns occupying my mind. Letting go, little by little, I entered the unknown—very scary and very liberating at the same time. I gained glimpses of understanding how my thoughts, when left unattended, created a false reality that I grabbed onto as real and followed like a dog in heat. My eyes and mind were opening.

Like a sculpture coming into focus, old personas, feelings of arrogance and inferiority, judgments of what was right and wrong, and my thinking I knew anything for sure, were falling away.

Nothing was certain. Life had it's own timing and delivered surprises – ready or not. Disasters such as: the fall of New York's Twin Towers in 2001, the Indonesian tsunami in 2004 and the 9. 0 earthquake in Japan in 2011 are dramatic reminders that life is a moment-to-moment, second-by-second unfolding on its own terms.

Each moment arises and right along with it a new perspective. When I'd use an old perception to assess or judge an event happening in the present moment, I wasn't allowing myself to see new possibilities. By not overlaying my thoughts and opinions from the past, I more clearly saw what was true in the new, present moment.

I was learning that perfection didn't mean having no faults or flaws. It meant seeing the perfection in everything just the way it is.

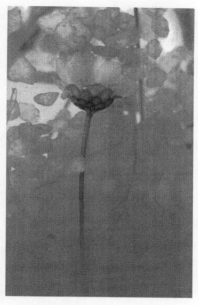

"I want to let you in on a little secret. There are no problems. Problems just mean the world isn't turning out the way you want it to. Everything is unfolding as it should."
~ROBERT ADAMS

II

What if your Problem's Not the Problem?

The First Practice

What if everything you consider to be a problem isn't a problem after all? What if everything that happens, whether it seems right or wrong or feels good or bad, is happening exactly the way it should? What if you knew that to be true with every fiber of your being? What would your life be like? Would it change?

When I first encountered this concept, it sounded like a conundrum. I couldn't make any sense of it. How could there be no problems? But my curiosity was peaked.

Seeing Through the Problem
In June of 2005 while enrolled in the Radiant Mind Training, this concept was offered to a group of well educated, spiritually wise, mature men and women. I sat and watched the concept challenged. Everyone seemed just as curious as I was and just as interested in understanding what was being posed. We were good students because Peter Fenner, founder of the Radiant Mind Training, was a great teacher. I'm not sure what was finally asked or said when I lit up, but I finally got it. I cracked the code to my old programming and saw what made a problem a problem – me.

Once I got it, like a kid with a new toy, or more accurately a spiritual seeker with a new tool, I began testing this "theory" on everything I labeled a problem. First I started with mere irritations. I noticed that when my computer malfunctioned or I forgot to save a file before shutting it down, I'd become incensed. Every time I had a difference of opinion with a customer service representative and didn't get my way, even after leaning heavily on "the customer is always right," I was reluctant to give in (making it a problem). When a crick would form in the back-yard hose, frustrated I'd try to whip it loose. I became aware how I stressed over these little things, making their contrary-to-my-liking, a problem. The energy I expended fighting reality was exhausting. That was the first eye-opener.

Once aware of my useless struggles, I stopped myself before the fight. When caught behind a slow driver on a single lane, two-way street on my way to an appointment, instead of getting irritated, I'd take a breath and remember I had a cell phone and could call if I was running late. When a cashier at the market was inefficient in my eyes, and taking more than the necessary time ringing up the customer in front of me, I'd take a breath and wait patiently. Each time I caught myself in the act of stressing over one of these or similar annoyances, I'd simply ask myself, *what if this wasn't a problem?* I realized that creating a problem was just a way of distracting myself from my discomfort with the way things were. By abolishing the notion that what didn't go my way was a "problem," I simply eliminated getting sidetracked by all the small frustrations, anger, hurt, etc.

Soon, all it took was a shift in my perception and more often than not, little inconveniences stopped rattling my cage. I was amazed at how this one simple adjustment to my attitude gave me a sense of peace and calm. I felt as if I'd awakened to a better part of myself. I shared this epiphany with everyone I knew.

Months later, still enrolled in the training, I was diagnosed with a lump in my thyroid. I had all the tests but the doctors couldn't determine if the lump was cancerous. They had to operate to find out for sure. I was shocked. I'd never had to be hospitalized overnight for anything except childbirth.

I had the operation and everything was fine—the lump was not cancerous. But during the process of preparing for surgery, I was told that if they had to remove the thyroid, I'd be on medication my whole life to regulate my metabolism. I know this is going to seem strange but because I have a strong aversion to taking supplements, I was more concerned with that fact than the possibility of having cancer. Maybe I was diverting my fear, but regardless, I was creating a problem by projecting my fear into the future based on my past experience with supplements. I was afraid that if I didn't take the medicine prescribed (which given my personality was a definite possibility), I'd have a lot of health problems. For an active person like myself, that thought was devastating.

Mulling over this dilemma, I heard the question arise, *What if this wasn't a problem*? By now I was familiar with this query but still working at it. I knew thinking something was a problem was what made it one. So how could I see this in another light? I suddenly felt a rush of air as if I were standing in a stuffy room and a window was opened. I got the "no problem" concept on a whole new level. I saw how most things that seem like a problem didn't have anything to do with the present moment. They only felt problematic based on past experience or by projecting a future possibility. In the present moment, the problem doesn't exist. In my case, I didn't yet know if I'd need to take the medication and wouldn't know for two weeks. Stressing out wasn't going to help. If everything went well, I wouldn't have to do anything. If it didn't, there'd be plenty of time to deal with the circumstances.

The point behind this example is universal. Worrying about worst-case scenarios and believing they're real creates stress. But stressing over future possibilities doesn't change the end result. It only causes the one who's stressing, anguish. Every time I get in a stressful situation and forget or ignore the question *what if this wasn't a problem,* I wind up miserable. Nothing positive comes out of it except maybe a reinforcement to remember the question.

It's not about denying the circumstances. It's about being with the affect of the situation as it currently presents itself. The present moment is the only thing we have any influence over.

My Arrogance Card was Revoked

Before I understood that thinking there is a problem is what actually creates one, I believed that if I did everything "right," life would reciprocate by giving me everything I wanted, exactly the way I wanted it. When that didn't work, I believed something was wrong; there *was* a problem. I felt a certain entitlement to having things go my way, and when they didn't, I'd get frustrated or confused. This belief made me see contrary situations as problems.

Extremely invested in life happening on my terms, I became a great problem solver and managed life so my desires came to fruition. I'd one-pointedly focus on what I wanted. If that didn't create results fast enough, I'd plow through all obstacles, not always gracefully nor thinking about what was best for all involved, until things worked out in my favor. I felt invincible.

Then, life handed me a perfectly designed customized event for *moi*. Unlike situations in the past, no matter what I did I couldn't see how to fix this one. Immediately, I jumped on the bandwagon of, "I've got a problem." Anyone could see that. In fact, everyone I told about my dilemma justified my position. (Fight for your limitations and they're yours.)

In 1996 I moved to Boulder, Colorado. I spent the first two years developing a small media sales training company. All my efforts dissolved overnight when a large publishing firm bought out all the small newspaper businesses that made up 90% of my clientele. Once the initial shock wore off, I knew I needed to change focus. No Problem. I decided to lean on a skill I'd developed prior to moving and create a program that brought community building into school classrooms. With a new shot of adrenalin, I forged ahead.

Knowing it might take a while to get started and needing immediate income, I placed a situation-wanted ad in the Denver Post touting a can-do-anything attitude. A woman named

Rita responded to the ad and after agreeing to take on her project and successfully negotiating my fee with her and her boss, Richard, I was hired. The plan was that I'd work from my home office except when delivering their product. *Perfect. I can develop my school project along with theirs, I thought.* This was how life worked. An obstacle arose and I worked my magic.

I discussed the details of employment with my sister, Linda, who warned me with, "You know what they say. If it seems too good to be true, it usually is." She was referring to all the perks—flying to the cities where my sons just happened to live (still don't know if that was a coincidence), being given a clothing allowance for when I met their affluent clients, my high salary, etc. I heard her, but feeling she was more cautious than I needed to be, I went ahead with my plans. I figured I had nothing to lose.

My training started the following week. Via phone, Rita walked me through the process. I'd find gold coins at the best price, purchase them with funds Richard would send me in advance, and deliver the gold to a location where he and his clients were meeting. It seemed easy and straightforward. Rita and I quickly developed a great rapport. I couldn't wait to meet her. She was due to fly in after the weekend.

For the next couple of weeks Rita reeled me in, finding good reasons to delay her trip to Boulder. Meanwhile I learned about getting the best price and the timing of the transactions since gold fluctuated daily. She was always busy taking care of her new life that included a troublesome stepdaughter whom she'd taken responsibility since her recent marriage. This, she explained, was the reason she needed to train someone to replace her. I would beep her and she'd return my calls promptly. I empathized with her tiresome shopping trips to the mall or other activities she endured with her 14-year old sidekick and she gushed with envy over the accessible hiking trails I took advantage of in Boulder. I felt I'd known Rita forever. Everything was moving along smoothly until the _ _ _ _ hit the fan.

Fast-forward three weeks. Having received a check for $224,000 to secure my first gold transaction, I proceeded by depositing it in an account I set up in my name the previous week. Once the check cleared, I issued a certified check to the gold dealer for the gold coins, secured another check for the private plane I'd fly in to take me to Arizona and wrote a third check to myself for my salary. The next day I flew on a Learjet to the designated private airport, handed the gold to a courier, and flew home—easy and exciting. I couldn't wait for the next assignment.

The following afternoon the doorbell rang and I found a Sherriff standing at my door, He showed me his badge and asked, "Are you Jasmyne Boswell?" Feeling a bit confused by his presence I stammered, "Yes." I felt his eyes bore into mine as he continued. "Did you know the check you deposited a couple of days ago was counterfeit?" I was stunned and couldn't respond. Still slightly in shock I opened the door and let him in.

As we walked to the dining room and sat down at the table, I reviewed the previous week's activities in my head. I remembered certain doubts—Rita postponing all her trips and the check showing up later than originally promised. *But wouldn't the bank have noticed if something was wrong with the check when they first saw it? They're the experts. Surely they'd be held responsible.* I felt sick. After relaying the details of my espionage, I could tell the Sherriff knew I'd been duped. But because I'd crossed state lines taking the gold to Arizona, the FBI became involved.

At that time if someone said, "There are no real problems" and looks could kill, they'd be dead. The fallout from the scam threw me into a world of attorneys and mediations. The bank was suing me for the $218,000 I withdrew from my new account to pay for the gold, the Learjet and my salary. I felt like a little kid lost in a grown-up's world. The feeling of having control over my life along with any prior confidence in my ability to make sound decisions vanished. My ego had been mashed into tiny, unrecognizable pieces. My arrogance card had been revoked.

Seeing Problems Everywhere

Problems were all I could see. I didn't have any work, I had to pay for attorneys I couldn't afford and my magical life seemed to be coming to an end. All my time was taken up in a world I knew nothing about. It wasn't that I didn't have tools at my disposal. I'd been on a dedicated personal growth and spiritual path for the past 25 years. I'd worked with both Jungian and Gestalt therapists, engaged in rage therapy, meditated, taken part in new age encounter experiences, sat with many guides who channeled the wisdom of out-of-body entities, journeyed with Shamans, studied Buddhism and followed Hindu Gurus. I considered myself somewhat conscious. But I wasn't yet privy to the idea that a problem was only a problem if I saw it as one.

Life hit me with a surprise curve ball, and I caved. Going from feeling like I was on my game to feeling like humpty dumpty who took a great fall, was devastating. My life was out of my control. For the six months it took to clear things up, I was stressed out, depressed and obsessed with thoughts about everything that could possibly happen, including losing my home. Even though I was out of work, I wouldn't even think of running another ad. The effects of this "too-good-to-be-true" offer definitely created what I perceived as a problem.

In retrospect I see that by thinking it was a problem, for months my attention was buried in thoughts of impotency and depression. I felt sick to my stomach most of the time as my mind kept producing one bad scenario after another and I accepted each one as a potential outcome. Thinking I had a problem exacerbated the situation and made me miserable and dysfunctional.

Like circumstances do, eventually they worked themselves out even if not exactly the way I hoped they would. After an intimidating mediation with the bank's attorneys, I finally found my strength. I still believed, even if they didn't agree, that the bank was more responsible for cashing the check than I was for depositing it. After convincing my attorney that this was so, she negotiated on those grounds and the bank settled, ending the suit for the $3300 I would have profited from the scam after attorney fees. The FBI stopped calling me and I gladly put this saga to rest.

If I'd known to ask myself the question, "What if this wasn't a problem," I still might have felt devastated. But that question brings with it a change in perception. Just for a moment, the old thinking stops, allowing a more present state of awareness to take its place. Without remorse for the past and fears projected on the future, it would have been easier to see what needed to be done and I could have diminished the fear and stress.

Nine years later when I grocked the concept, *"What if your Problem's not the Problem,"* I couldn't help wishing I'd come across it a few years back. But life happens on its terms – not ours. Having the illusion of being in control is a false safety net that can be pulled out from under us at any time. In truth, we don't have a clue what the next moment will bring.

Life-changing antics happen every day. People lose their homes that burn to the ground in unpredictable fires, parents lose a young child due to a sudden illness or accident, and individuals devastated by the stock market crash and scams such as Enron and Madoff, lose their life savings. If you've lived for any length of time, I'm sure you can come up with your own list of untimely events.

Fear and Problems

When caught in fear of loss, whether its of a relationship, money, comfort or any form of annihilation, we are built for survival, so our minds work overtime to bring us back to some sense of order so we can feel in control. Since we don't have control over reality, either in the form of human nature or Mother Nature, learning to befriend feeling out of control, or what we consider a problem, is helpful. I've found it to be a life preserver.

I'm sure you've heard it said, "If you want to see God laugh, tell Her your plans." Even so, plan we do. And, I did.

I went on a camping trip with my friend Claire to Lana'i, one of the closest Hawaiian Islands to Maui. It's about a 45-minute ferry ride from the harbor in Lahaina, a town on the west side of the island. The 9:00 a.m. ferry ride was blissful.

She and I sat on the top deck and cruised with the cool ocean spray kissing our faces and the crisp sea breeze blowing our hair. What a view! We watched the West Maui Mountains disappear and the harbor grow smaller and smaller until it practically faded away.

We were going to take just a day trip to the island. But when I relayed my intense fear of getting seasick, which normally kept me away from boats altogether, and my apprehension of ferrying back in the late afternoon noted for rougher ocean conditions, Claire agreed to camp over for one night. The moment we started putting up our tent we knew we'd stay for two; too much work and too much to explore for one day.

Though the weather was touch-and-go, snorkeling in the beautiful clear bay, great walks along the cliffs, perusing the quaint city of Lanai and dinners at the luxurious Four Seasons Hotel within walking distance of the campground made up for any discomfort – as long as we were on land.

Our second day there we ran into a woman who was taking the afternoon ferry back to Maui. She expressed her concern, referencing the winds that had picked up in the past few hours. I secretly congratulated myself for choosing a morning departure. Mother Nature, however, had a surprise in store for the following day, and a smooth ride back wasn't it.

The winds continued to pickup during the night. In the morning after Claire and I broke camp and packed up, even the water in the bay donned white caps. I had to teach the following day; so waiting for smoother seas wasn't an option. I was going to have to walk my talk, not see this as a problem, and be with what was.

We boarded the ferry, and same as the way over, Claire and I made our way with other passengers to the top deck. I always preferred the fresh air to the inside cabins. It seemed to help ward off nausea. We were barely seated when one of the crewmen climbed the metal staircase to greet us. Instead of the usual welcome aboard he announced, "There'll be no outside seating due to weather conditions." Disappointed, many of us questioned him, airing our strong preference for sitting outdoors." Believe me," he assured us, "you'll be thanking me in the end." Then came the captain's broadcast over the loudspeaker. "We're in for a rough ride. Everyone take a seat inside the cabins and hold on to any small children. Those with a tendency toward seasickness may want to sit on the bottom level at the rear of the boat." *Oh no,*

I thought, *I'm about to live my worst nightmare.* I took a deep breath, gave Claire a fearful look and followed the others descending the metal staircase for the lower deck. I sat down and turned sideways so I could grip the high backs of both my seat and the one in front of me.

As we departed the dock, paper bags were handed out to those who thought they might need one. I graciously accepted. I recited to myself, *there are no problems.* Still, I tightened my grip as the ferry took off. *I can endure anything for 45 minutes* I consoled myself. The ferry bobbed forward and back, side-to-side, slapping the water repeatedly as it rode the waves. The immediate tossing about was discouraging as we were still partially protected in the bay and hadn't yet entered open seas.

"Look at the height of that spray," exclaimed Claire excitedly, attempting some small talk to ease my worries. I could tell she wanted to make me feel better but I had enough on my hands. "I can't talk now. I'm doing all I can to manage myself," I said loudly as I let out a deep breath, cringing with the rise and crashing descent. The sound of the boat hitting the water was deafening.

I could feel the tension building in my arms and shoulders as conditions worsened. I felt completely out of control. Not much I could do about it. As the saying goes, "Nowhere to run, nowhere to hide." Then came the thought, *this is only a problem if you make it one*. Amazingly, that thought broke through my conditioned reaction.

Having spent the last fifteen minutes wincing and contracting as the intense rock'n and roll'n and bouncing about continued, I had to admit that I wasn't the slightest bit nauseous. With that realization, my anxiety over being sick subsided. *Okay so that's not a problem*. With that bit of relief I began to wonder if I could relax my body. I consciously dropped my shoulders and released my now tired hip and leg muscles. Even sitting down they were working overtime. With the next rise we smacked hard on the water. I looked around. I noticed some people talking while others looked out the window. There were a few who looked worried, but they were in the minority.

I loosened my grip on the seats. *No problem*, I kept thinking. Then another thought arose, *what would it be like to just sit with your hands in your lap*? (Writing this I'm noticing how not focusing on this as a problem changed my internal dialogue). Taking it slowly, I let go with my left hand and tried to stay relaxed while still flinching as the boat took another big wave. I noticed I was somewhat reluctant to give in so easily, but once I relaxed, I had to admit it wasn't that bad.

Then another thought entered my mind. *Could you enjoy the ride?* Hmmm. Slowly, I dropped my other arm to my side and allowed my body to roll with the motion of the sea. Being with every moment just as it was happening, I felt extremely alive. I looked at Claire and said, "This isn't as bad as I thought it'd be." She smiled and said, "It's definitely a rough ride." And it was. Still, I had been unnecessarily suffering during the first part of it.

My fear felt real based on past experiences and future projections and that's where the problem was alive. I couldn't change the conditions of the stormy sea. But by being present with what was, the reality of what I believed would be horrific, or a problem, shifted.

Looking back at my behavior and beliefs around the scam mentioned earlier in this chapter, I see how my knee-jerk, fear reaction made the situation seem insurmountable. My fear over what the bank could do to me, my worrying over the loss of money, my doubt that I could ever trust myself or anyone else again were projected thoughts that led me down a dark tunnel of depression. Some of those thoughts were true. I was losing money and I didn't know what the bank could do. But as in the case of the ferry ride, where I separated the fear from reality and dealt with what was right in front of me on it's terms, I was able to access the wisdom of the present moment and my suffering was minimized. There wasn't a problem at hand, just a situation I needed to pay attention to.

I can't say I will fearlessly run toward the next boat heading out on a stormy sea. But the experience of consciously meeting my fear and discomfort by being with it instead of resisting it, saved me from a huge amount of stress that allowed me to eventually enjoy the ride. This same conscious, step-by-step scrutiny can be applied to any situation we label a problem. The truth and wisdom is in the potent presence.

Seduction of Problem Solving
For those of us with minds that like to be busy, problem solving can be very seductive and satisfying. It gives the mind something new to obsess about and chew upon. Without realizing it, we can live our lives from problem to problem and even delight in sharing them with those around us. We dramatize and create great

stories trying to fix ourselves, others, systems, countries, anything we *think* needs to be different than it is. Unconsciously or consciously we keep finding something wrong with the way things are to satisfy our need for keeping busy. We repeat the same pattern over and over again with varying story lines.

Finding solutions to mysteries, espionage, betrayal, kidnapping, and other calamities comprise a big percentage of our entertainment; i.e. television shows such as C.S.I, films like "The Tourist" and books like the Da Vinci Code. A problem sets the scene and we watch or read attentively as the hero or heroine rises to the occasion and wins the battle. The more dramatic the plot, the more intensely we feel the resolve. That kind of entertainment can be a great escape from our own life and a nice place to visit. But when that intensity filters into daily living, it is time and energy consumed in ways that are debilitating to the health of our body, mind and spirit.

Life is like a Jigsaw Puzzle

Life can be likened to a jigsaw puzzle. When sitting down to put a puzzle together, we simply search for the piece that fits and connect it to another. We continue doing this and each step miraculously informs the next, until *viola* the puzzle takes its final shape. If we thought something was wrong every time a piece didn't fit another one and started strategizing how to change that piece to fit, we'd become obsessed, stressed out and have to work much harder to accomplish an end result; or give up. However, working it step-by-step, we discover a solution in each moment.

We don't know how our behavior has a hold on us until we put our lives under a microscope. When we do, we become conscious of how we create problems out of situations simply because they aren't going in the direction we desire. Changing our ways is not easy. But it's also not that difficult if, like with a jigsaw puzzle, we take each step, one moment at a time.

The minute we see that what we're calling a problem isn't a problem our experience shifts. Those few words, *what if the problem's not the problem*, can transform the way we see and feel about any troubling situation and can save us from a lot of body/mind stress and bring us peace.

Whenever I'm feeling something should be different than it is, I also become aware of the tensing of my muscles. If someone took a picture of me at that moment, I'm sure I'd look years older. When I change from thinking something is a problem to seeing it for what it is (a' la the ferry ride from Lana'i), I relax. This makes it easier to determine what, if anything, I need to do. Eliminating this kind of stress is a youth elixir in itself.

When We Play God
The more we create conflict with ourselves or others by thinking that what's happening shouldn't be, the more we're at war with ourselves. In effect we're saying, "We know better."

Have you seen the film, "Bruce Almighty," starring Jim Carey, Morgan Freeman and Jennifer Aniston? In the film, Morgan Freeman, who plays God, hands his role over to Jim Carey to show him that the job isn't as easy as he thinks it is. Jim Carey now has the power to solve all the world's problems. We soon see that he lacks the wisdom or the "broad view" to foresee the consequences of his actions.

First, he lets everyone win the lottery and, of course, there's a rush on the banks and not enough money to go around. But my favorite moment was when he changed the moon cycle so it would be full on the evening he wanted to seduce Jennifer Aniston. The following day, the news reported tsunamis and earthquakes in Asia. Every action does have a reaction. We simply don't sit high enough to judge what's right and wrong or to know how everything is interconnected.

When we break away from automatically seeing a situation as a problem when something goes contrary to our thinking, we are more likely to approach life inquisitively. We then enter a dimension of curiosity and discovery. From that perspective we are open to all possibilities. Then, problems don't exist. There are simply situations calling for our attention. Our presence allows us to benefit from a myriad of subtleties that make life easier and a lot more fun.

Key Points:

1: Every time you think something is a problem, ask yourself, "What if this wasn't a problem?"

2. It's the small everyday frustrations we label problems that cause built-up stress – master these and the big ones will be easier to manage.

3: A problem is simply a situation that needs our attention.

4: Life is like a jigsaw puzzle – each step informs the next.

5. We don't sit high enough to judge.

Inquiries:

1: What if the problem's not the problem?
2: Am I distracting myself by creating a problem? If so, how?
3: Am I involved in thoughts of past and/or future?
4: Do I create stress in my body/mind fighting with reality?

Exercise:

You can do this exercise either on your own by writing down your responses or in a group appointing a scribe.

Think of a current situation you consider a problem.

1. Write about the problem as you see it.
2. Then write down what you're doing to change it.
3. Ask yourself, "Is there any way I'm trying to manipulate reality to suit my wants and needs?" If so, write down how.
4. Then ask yourself, "What would it look like if I didn't try to change the situation and instead dealt with it on its terms?" In other words, how might you change your attitude and/or actions to meet the experience just as it is?

*"The **obvious** is that which is never seen until someone expresses it simply."*
~KAHLIL GIBRAN

III

Doing What's Obvious

The Second Practice

You know the feeling you get when you're trying to figure something out and someone points you toward a solution that's been right in front you all along? That's what this practice is like, only something within you is doing the pointing. Your only requirement is to pay attention to that subtle, steady voice or feeling within. Like fine-tuning the dial on a radio station to get beyond the static for clear reception, becoming skilled at doing what's obvious takes attuning your senses to the clarity and wisdom that lies just beyond the chattering mind. I found that once I carved a path to its whereabouts, I could access it more easily and life became simpler.

Understanding how the Mind Works

The mind constantly produces thoughts. That's its job. It has answers or comments for just about everything. When we make a decision, get concerned, or are at a choice point, it offers a multitude of suggestions. We rely on it to pull stored information from our memory bank to help us navigate life. We rely on it to read, to learn and engage it for work and play activities. It's a great tool and for the most part it's there when we need it. However, unlike other tools that we put away when we finish a task, our mind doesn't sit quietly on the shelf awaiting our next invitation.

Instead, it likes center stage. Invited or not it vies for our attention with worries and details about our past and opportunities for our future, succeeding to distract us more than not. This leaves little space or time for being fully present. Our mind is persistent and relentless. Until we see it for what it is – a machine that produces thoughts, non-stop with no off switch - we're at its mercy. Once we understand how it works, we can learn to pick it up or put it on the shelf, *like a good tool*, until *we* decide it's needed.

Being taken in by mind is like going to the movies. Think about the last time you got immersed in a great film. While engrossed, were you saying to yourself, "This is only a movie?" If it was a good one, you probably got lost in it. But when the film ended and the lights went on, you walked out of the theater knowing the film was a story projected on a screen.

We are captured by our thoughts in the same way. Normally, when our thoughts are playing out some scenario, we don't say, "Oh those are just my thoughts." Instead, we buy into their reality. But once the light of awareness goes on, we're not as easily swept away nor do we automatically accept our thoughts for the truth.

Noticing how I allowed my thoughts to play me like a puppet, I started watching them more closely. I saw how they seduced me into their rich tapestry of questions, answers, opinions and stories. Like the most intimate lover, they knew me well and pulled my strings. They lured and provoked me at their whim. When not consciously aware, like an addict, I was enslaved to their romantic, intelligent and dramatic quality. I was under their spell.

Taken for a Ride

One evening during a group meditation, aware that I was unable to stop following my thoughts, I consciously decided to give in. I watched every thought flow freely with pure fascination. They were brilliant and had the ability to propel me into feelings, conversations or plans for the future, full of visual affects and story lines, captivating me like a kid entering Disneyland for the first time.

My thought stream went like this: Playing on a conversation I overheard earlier in the evening about a group of friends going to swim with the whales, my mind conjured up a story. *Everyone is going swimming with the whales. Why haven't you heard about it? Maybe you won't be invited.* I listened to one set of thoughts argue with a placating version of myself. *I won't be able to go any way because I'll be teaching.* The argument continued, *but they didn't even think to pick a day when you could go.* It continued along those lines until my newly acquired cat, Ku'ulei (Hawaiian for sweetheart) popped in and took center stage. *I could see his darling face, and that cute little pink nose. Next a memory popped in of my squirming earlier that day when I saw him play with his latest catch, a gecko. I felt the immensity of my love for him even though he grossed me out. Then I got caught up in another thought of my upcoming trip to the mainland and wondered if I could really leave my precious kitty for three weeks when I went to California. It would be hard to find someone who'd give him the attention I would.* Off on another tangent, my mind took me to California. *I could almost taste the Brie, hard rolls and dark, rich coffee at the Rose Café.* The thoughts went on and on, one lending itself to another until the chimes rang quietly three times bringing my awareness back into the room.

When I opened my eyes, very little if anything had changed. Everyone in the group was still sitting in the same seats as when we began and looking at the clock on the far wall, I saw that only 20 minutes had passed. I silently laughed seeing my mind not only as an alluring source of entertainment, but as a clever player that fed me exactly what it knew would grab my attention and captivate me.

That was a great teaching. My mind created a reality all its own. If I let myself believe those thoughts without being consciously aware of their fabrication, I could easily feel hurt thinking I was being left out of a whale adventure and stress over my cat being lonely. I could also give unnecessary attention to imagined situations on my future trip to California. If I let them, my thoughts could talk me into believing anything. ***To get to what's obvious and the optimum choice in any given moment I had to learn to see and listen beyond the distraction of superfluous thoughts.***

Allowing myself to get wrapped in needless internal dialogue was fine as an experiment, but I didn't want to be at my mind's beck and call when I sat to meditate or wanted to focus on what was in front of me. It was too distracting. I wanted the option of listening to thought *or* the other intelligent centers and senses that were available from within.

Having been in the advertising business for many years, I knew how important it was to know one's competition. If I wanted to shift my attention from random thinking to a deeper wisdom, I needed to become more aware of how and when I became distracted by mind.

Consciously listening to our thoughts and learning to observe them takes practice. Just like when watching a film, any time we're absorbed in thought, we're not present to much else. When unaware of how we habitually follow thought, we are more likely to slide into automatic habits. Automatic responses come in handy for what we might call mindless actions such as brushing our teeth, making our bed or starting our car. But to be at choice takes being conscious of how we default to automatic pilot and how we unconsciously follow thought. When we automatically follow thought, we both prevent ourselves from taking risks, i.e.: worrying if someone we don't want to bump into will see us if we . . . , or hold ourselves back from asking for a promotion, or make excuses for learning how to play a new instrument. Thoughts of excitement such as: making a purchase before checking our finances or leaving a relationship for greener pastures without giving the consequences our full attention, can also cause unnecessary suffering. Our thoughts can talk us into or out of situations and lead us around by a leash if we're not aware.

Finding a Needle in a Haystack
Practicing awareness is key to doing what's obvious. Without awareness, the only reality we're keyed into is the one thought offers. When we live in the moment, we're allowing ourselves to connect to fresh insights. That is how we allow the subtle messages to get

through, pointing us to the obvious thing to do. The mind then becomes a backdrop until *we decide* to call on its strength.

As witness to my thoughts, I became aware of how they justified my every move. When I sat down at the computer first thing in the morning, one set of thoughts berated me for that habit. *What about meditating or doing Qigong first? The computer is no way to start the day.* Another thought contradicted the first one; "*Of course you have to turn on your computer first thing and check your emails. What if a client is trying to reach you or if a new client sent an inquiry?*" *You haven't had any new clients yet this month and your coaching load is low.* Each thought engaged another. One scolded while one very cleverly validated my need to feel responsible playing on my fear of scarcity. I observed similar relationships between other thoughts and justifications. Again I was amazed at how following thoughts as if they were real kept me emotionally involved, following a story that usually had to do with fear about something – loss, embarrassment, insecurity . . .

Learning to distinguish thoughts produced randomly or induced by fear from those that represent the truth of the moment is an acquired skill that at first can be like, as the saying goes, "trying to find a needle in a haystack."

I was staying in the adjacent guesthouse of the home where the Radiant Mind training was held. Peter, our teacher, was staying in an extra room in the house. One morning while standing in the kitchen I became aware of how I distinguished the difference between fear thoughts and those producing the truth.

To the left of the kitchen was a large, enclosed room with a swimming pool and hot tub. Those staying on the property had a morning ritual of going into the Jacuzzi before breakfast. I started to follow the others on cue but feeling a slight resistance from within, I stopped. ***That was the first and most important step. Stopping brought me out of autopilot and allowed me to focus within.*** As the others walked past me I asked myself out loud, "Do you really want to go?" I stood quietly and listened for an answer. Again, speaking out loud, I voiced my response, "No, I don't." I realized what I really wanted to do was take a shower and get ready for the morning session. Once I stopped and listened, the simple truth delivered itself and with it came a sense of resolution.

Unbeknownst to me, Peter was in earshot of my little expose' and said with a delighted surprise in his voice, "You got your answer without trying to figure it out." I turned around and saw him standing behind me. "Yes, I got a very clear *No.*"

Peter's sharing what he observed had me reflect on my actions and I realized that's how I'd been getting to the truth for years. When just beginning a path toward consciousness, I heard one of my teachers say, "If you're not getting a yes, then it's a no." He further explained, "Simply ask yourself a yes or no question. Then listen carefully. Which one feels stronger—the yes or the no? If you don't get a definitive answer, then for the time being it's a no." His advice served me well and even though not always consciously, I'd been using it ever since.

The practice of Doing What's Obvious took that practice a bit further, but the principle was the same. When I stop following thought for a moment and listen, suddenly there's space for the deepest truth to make itself known. The stopping is about quieting random thinking and not getting distracted by all the more subjective thoughts that in the past would have me go along with the crowd. Stopping helped me find the truth in *that* present moment. That truth always prevents me from vacillating and points me to the wisdom that's presenting itself in the moment; in this particular moment that truth was to take a shower and get ready. Not very dramatic; but each time I stop and listen and follow that subtle direction, I bring more authenticity into my actions.

Embracing Fear

There are contrasting views on whether thought always precedes a feeling or whether it is possible for feelings to precede thought. My personal experience leads me to believe that a majority of the time I think of something, be it disturbing or elating, and an emotion of pain or pleasure follows. Therefore, when I feel an emotion such as fear, I can usually trace it back to a troublesome thought.

For instance: On one particular occasion I felt a tightening in my stomach and associated that contraction with fear. Wondering where it came from I asked myself, *what were you thinking just before you became aware of that feeling?* Using my mind to trace a previous thought process I realized I'd been focused on my dwindling bank account due to excessive car repairs that month. *Ah,* I thought and asked myself, *is that really a problem?* That Inquiry prompted me to review my current finances and realize it wasn't. I would be getting sufficient funds at the end of the month to cover all my expenses. If the fear had been justified, the inquiry would've let me know I needed to pay attention.

Another time I felt a wave of nervous energy run through my body. Again I asked myself, *what happened just before that feeling came on?* I remembered having a conversation with a client and was uncomfortable because I couldn't get a good read on how that person felt about my offer.

In both cases the fear came from an automatic response, patterns I fell into when faced with unscheduled expenses and unknown reactions. Fear couldn't upset me once I saw what provoked it and that it wasn't based on a present reality.

Prior to being conscious of how many of my fears started from a thought about some imagined or exaggerated consequence, my fear could dominate my life. Like a cloudy sky, it obscured the light of awareness – my inner wisdom. I'd allowed emotionally induced stories to build, causing my body and mind to fill with negative feelings and thoughts. It was like taking a horrifying role in a play except I wasn't being paid to act. It was my life and I couldn't simply walk off the set at the end of the day. Before I knew to trace feelings to thoughts, my fear had free reign. Then just like in a horror film when the villain catches the victim, there was no other reality available.

When you can't seem to trace your fear to a particular thought, it might take longer to find its source and let go. But inquiry is still the key. I remember after the scam I mentioned in the second chapter, I was in a very dark place. There were so many streams of thought plunging me into despair that I couldn't find their inception. I simply had to immerse myself in the feeling of anguish to get clarity. As I consciously allowed myself to focus all my attention and feel the discomfort, my entire body contracted. I felt a wave of shame engulf me. My pride had taken a big hit. Embracing or feeling my fear allowed me to release the clenching in my body as a softer presence shared the space of fear. I suddenly felt compassion for myself. My body relaxed and I had a better understanding of what I was going through. With that broader perspective I eventually opened to other possibilities.

By focusing on the sensations in the body, we shift our awareness away from the thoughts that often produce inaccurate motives for what is really going on. This helps us get beyond the chatter to allow the intelligence of the body to speak without interference from emotionally provoked stories.

Whether following the thought or the feeling, once I discover the root cause of a troubling emotion, I am free. Instead of getting caught up in future consequences that might not have any volition and are usually more exaggerated than reality, I simply change my perspective.

Hearing the Obvious

I like to think of the thought delivering the 'obvious' as one that speaks from an impartial aspect of myself, one that somehow knows what's best. It seems to have more of an eagle-eye view or broader perspective of current circumstances and takes in more than just a personal preference or an impulse to maintain comfort at all cost.

Because these obvious directives aren't necessarily there to make us feel better, they aren't always easy to follow. They can elicit anxiety when their direction advises an action or risk that warrants undesirable change.

One afternoon in 1996 I had a realization that I wasn't going to be with my fiancée any longer. This insight in the same unwavering way as the "*no*" (regarding the morning Jacuzzi ritual with friends) delivered a felt sense that let me know our relationship was on its way out. My stomach knotted up. All my fears rose to the surface. My fiancée, Michael, and I had moved to Estes Park, Colorado a year before and were living on a 103-acre ranch. He was the love of my life. I'd given up my work and my life in California to pursue our dream of starting a community. I didn't want to abandon our plans or my dreams. But the 'obvious' wasn't necessarily concerned with my desire to keep on a planned course. It took a number of months for the whole truth to unfold and for me to take action.

I won't go into all the emotions that went along with leaving Michael. I think it's sufficient to say that if written, the torment would have made a first rate romance novel. Breaking away from all my emotional attachments felt devastating and at the same time, right. Separated, each of our life paths took us in a more authentic direction. Luckily our love survived and we remain best of friends.

Entre into the flow of life
Once I learned to hear the voice that delivered the obvious, I started depending on it to make all my decisions. Paying attention, it immediately became apparent that when making most decisions I grabbed on to my logical mind's approach. I strongly favored efficiency – a distinct family trait I'd adopted for getting things done quickly and *"the right way."* Watching myself lean toward doing everything in the most orderly fashion, from running errands to planning the flow of my day, I noticed my automatic tendency to ignore or push away any feeling or instinct that got in the way. If it was efficient and got me what I wanted, how could it be *wrong*?

In 2006 I moved from Boulder, Colorado to Maui. That move was the last thing I ever thought I wanted. Even though Maui is paradise personified and I loved visiting there often, I didn't feel ready to live that far from my family, friends and the Radiant Mind conscious community. But after returning from a visit the end of February that year, as hard as I tried to ignore it, the directive from within to move grew to a mammoth proportion and trying to fight it was like trying to swim the Colorado River upstream during spring melt. Mother Maui was calling me back and she meant business. I'd felt finished with Boulder for a while, but *Maui*?

For a week or so I sat with the idea of moving, listening to my mind go back and forth. *Warm weather and the beach year round, your best friend lives on-island, something new and different – but your eldest son, Robb, lives in Boulder, your spiritual community here is growing, you can drive to New Mexico where other close friends and your godsons live, both your sisters are only a short plane ride away, your clients know your work, you'll have to start all over.* No matter how my mind argued to steer me away from Maui or lure me to it, in the end neither side made my decision. It was something deeper. I recognized the feeling from past experiences when a big shift in my life was beckoning. It could not be ignored. Once I surrendered, waiting seemed out of the question and I set my sights on August or September.

Suddenly there was a lot to do, giving me great fuel to engage this practice. I started going into my automatic mindset of forging ahead and caught myself. Instead, I stopped and listened for an inner message trying not to mastermind the whole process at once. I sold my house a couple of years before, so owning fewer assets was in my favor.

Deciding what I'd take, what to sell and what my son might want was the obvious first step. My piano was first on my list. A thought arose, *put a for sale sign on your piano so those coming to look at your place will know it's for sale.* The owners of the town home I lived in put it on the market when I told them I'd be leaving late summer. *Not yet* came another thought. I felt the difference immediately. The *not yet* was emotionally charged while the *put-a-for-sale-sign on the piano* just stated an action. I decided to go with the sign and see what happened. Within a week, one of the realtors showing the property left a note on the piano while I was out, asking me to give her a call. She wound up buying the piano for her son and asked if I would hold it until the end of June so she could surprise him with it for his birthday. She paid up front and I got to use it almost the entire time I was there.

Next I heard *find out about selling the lease on your car*. I loved my car. I didn't follow that advice at first. Instead I checked on shipping fees and found they were outrageous, especially if I didn't stay and had to ship it back. Once that was settled, another thought arose. *What if the lease sells right away and you don't have a car for the next few months?* Recognizing the tone, I could tell the latter thought played on my fear of loss and I decided to relax and follow the message that came without a lot of fanfare. Long story short, this worked out much like the piano. The paperwork for transfer-of-ownership to the new owners went through the afternoon before the day I left Boulder. Although I had to talk myself through my nervousness that it wouldn't go through in time, I could not have planned it any better.

The process I was following intuitively showed me the most obvious next step. I just had to keep my awareness off the thoughts producing fear and attachment. I started feeling the liberation of doing what was obvious and being present to the moment. I also saw the wisdom in, "*The mind is a great servant but a poor master.*"

Paying attention, each next step revealed itself with perfect timing. When multiple choices arose such as, *you should stay till September 13th for your friend Jeff's wedding* and right behind it came *get to Maui before Labor Day so you can get a jump-start on your business*, I let the options volley back and forth until one that was simple and clear stood out and didn't waver. Following the straightforward prompts to action, I alleviated the confusion, stress and overwhelm of taking on everything at once. This practice left a lot of spaciousness for handling all the logistics. I was experiencing the meaning of having the wind at your back.

With all the particulars for the move under way, I focused on a business for Maui. My mind was having a field day with *how do you make money on-island?* Not financially independent, I had to create a quick-start business to support myself. And like most resort islands, the year-round population was small in comparison to many mainland cities and the cost of living was high. My current business would not transfer easily to island style.

This "how" thought could have brought the move to a stop. However, in the process of observing my actions I realized that when making a decision with my mind's logical thinking, that same logical process could just as easily talk me out of it. If instead, I paid attention to a decision that revealed itself, all the rational arguments didn't change that. So when my mind started second-guessing the move based on finances, at first I got caught up in the question *am I nuts for thinking I can make it on my finances?* But in the end, ***I trusted the process I was learning - stop, listen, wait for the simple direction and trust what's most obvious.***

The original calling that prodded me to make the move in the first place was strong and I had to stand back and allow all the obstacles to rise and fall, as I stayed present to the moment-by-moment truth as it presented itself. Just like with the car and piano, I knew when it was time to redo my website for my next business venture on Maui and when to book my flight. I finished designing business cards, came up with a plan for launching my new business by September 1st and in perfect harmony I landed on Maui August 6, 2006.

Everything worked out more easily than I could have imagined. By surrendering and doing what was obvious in the moment, my chatty mind had less of a hold on me. Without my allegiance, it couldn't lure me into all my fear places. Instead, focusing my attention beyond my mind's chatter, my impulse to push the river or get stuck in fear was replaced by patience, ease and eventually awe. Everything managed to get done without stressing or putting myself in wonder-woman mode. It was the most stress-free transition I'd ever made. Five years later I am still calling Maui my home.

Seeing that this practice worked during a major transition just as it did with the smaller, every day decisions without creating a lot of drama, was a thrill. As I look back and see the synchronicity of events and how everything presented itself in perfect timing without my logical, willful intention, it makes me wonder if what I call *"my life,"* actually has a life of its own. All the familiar sayings, "Go with the flow," "Ride the horse in the direction it's going," "What resists, persists," all point to this simple way of being.

What also became obvious when I eliminated the stress and fear from running my life was that I had fewer ups and downs. Dramas or distractions I created by following thoughts that only fabricated a reality that made me suffer greatly, diminished. With that, a certain amount of excitement I derived from being on edge also subsided.

At first I was relieved. After a while, it put my ego on tilt. Like Joseph Campbell's never ending hero's journey, my journey continued, peeling off layer after layer of conditioned beliefs and responses. Still enrolled in the Radiant Mind Course and commuting to Boulder for the retreat weekends, I was supported in my quest for peace. The third practice helped me further understand my restless mind, addressing my tilted ego.

Key points:
- Become aware of your thoughts
- Notice automatic actions and responses.
- Stop, wait and listen for the yes, no or the thought with little fanfare.
- Listen beyond the chattering mind to what's obvious.

Inquiries:

1. How much authority am I giving to my thoughts?
2. Am I allowing myself to be manipulated by random thinking? Do I follow my thoughts automatically without questioning their validity?
3. Do I STOP, WAIT and LISTEN for unwavering guidance before I act?
4. The inner wisdom messenger speaks with very little emotion. It is very direct. Am I aware of the difference between that voice and the voice of preferences?

Exercise:

You can do this exercise either on your own by writing your responses, with another as scribe or in a group appointing a scribe.

Are you your own authority or are you automatically believing and following unexamined thinking? Sit with this question for a moment.

Next time you need to make a decision, observe your thoughts and allow them to be just as they are – you don't have to immediately engage them. Breathe and become present.

1. Allowing any automatic reactions to settle down, listen for a non-emotional, inner voice that speaks simply and directly. If it's a yes/no question, ask yourself which response, the yes or the no, feels stronger? As best you can, clear your mind of personal preference and follow the strongest response.

2. If the words or messages you receive create fear, follow that fear to a thought or feeling that might have triggered that response. Ask yourself, "Is this fear based on reality?" If it is, allow that feeling of fear to guide you to what needs to be done. Unless there's imminent danger, that fear is usually based on past experience and won't hurt you in this moment. Let it inform you. If the fear is not real, see if you can let go and follow your guidance. It takes practice to hear and trust that steady voice within.

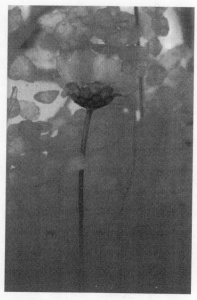

"Peace of mind is experienced when the stormy waves of the mind quell down."
~REMEZ SASSON

IV

Being Complete in the Moment

The Third Practice

If you want to know peace of mind, you'll find it by being complete in every moment. Being complete is as much of a guarantee as you'll find anywhere. When you're complete, your mind is quiet. And just like you go on holiday to get away from daily routines, being complete gives you a vacation from the busyness of mind. You're relieved of all the *how abouts, what ifs, the if only(s), the should haves* and all their cousins.

So what's necessary to be complete? Bringing your full awareness to what's showing up in the present moment. When we're present, we're not thinking about what we're going to do tomorrow nor reminiscing about what we did or should have done yesterday. We're simply in the moment that's right in front of us, NOW. And when we're present in that moment, we're complete. Nothing from the past or the future is needed or pulling on our attention.

There's nothing new about this viewpoint, but to live it is easier said than done. If it were easy, we'd have taken the advice of Ram Daas in the 70s and *"Be Here Now."* There would be no problems, we would only do what was obvious and naturally be complete in every moment.

But our minds like to wander. Have you every noticed that when you're lost in thought you literally don't see what's right in front of you? Instead, you're absorbed in whatever you're thinking. That's why so many of us share the similar, rather spooky experience of driving our car and when seduced by a thought, forget we're driving. Once we let go of the thought and again our eyes meet the road, we find ourselves wondering how we got from where we last remembered we were to where we are now. This distractive thinking usually involves everything past and future even though we can't do anything about them at present.

Contemplating this third practice I reflected on a retreat I attended in 1994 in Santa Fe, New Mexico. During mealtime we ate our meals in silence, focusing our attention first on each fork or spoonful of food we put in our mouth, then on the chewing, then the swallowing. When we walked, our attention was directed to the feel of our heel then our toe touching the earth and then the other foot lifting off the ground, etc. With that full attention on what we were doing, there was little chance for the mind to drift.

As profound as being present in every moment was, after the 10-day retreat ended, I went back to my life and my mind happily got back on its more familiar ground. Being present is not something we get good at and never have to think about again. If being present is important to us, it's something we keep coming back to when we catch ourselves trailing off in thought. Because this practice is so easy to understand, it's hard to imagine how challenging it can be to master. Becoming aware of how we wander from the present shows us how often we habitually stray.

Practicing Presence

Baldwin Beach is one of my favorite places on Maui's North Shore. You can walk the four-mile round-trip stretch, your feet never leaving sand the entire time. Unlike the beaches on the South and West side of the island, the surf is more active. The thwack of the waves crashing on the sandy shore is practically the only sound you hear.

On a clear day, the water ranges from shades of turquoise to midnight blue. Walking in one direction, you face the distant West Maui Mountains that more often than not are mystically capped in white, billowy clouds. It's always breathtaking but toward sunset, when the sun's rays penetrate the clouds and giant-like wings of diffused light reach toward the ocean floor, the view is spellbinding.

Walking in the opposite direction, you face the rainy side of the island dressed with jutting rocks and swaying palm trees. Often a vibrant rainbow, sometimes doubled, can be seen framing the scene like a picture perfect postcard. A view that exquisite would undoubtedly capture anyone's full attention keeping one glued to the present moment. At least you'd think so.

With this practice in mind, I'd go to the beach with full intention of being present to all the beauty it offers. I'd walk along watching how often my thoughts took me away from the moment. More often than not, instead of looking at the water or mountains, I'd become aware of being lost in thought. I'd purposefully focus on seeing the water. Pretty soon my sight would come back to the water and I'd realize I'd lost the connection while thoughts about stopping at the store on my way home or remembering something I'd forgotten to do wooed me. Again I'd set my intention and focus on the mountain. I'd take in the heavy mist draping the jagged peaks and pretty soon, same thing. Instead of seeing the mountain, I'd be reminiscing about a conversation I'd had on the phone earlier that day. Over and over again the present moment disappeared while I planned or reminisced. My intention of keeping my mind focused was overridden.

Continuing to play with this practice, I noticed there were certain activities that almost always got my full attention and stopped me from thinking about what was next or unfinished. These activities are universal—making love, laughing, rapt in conversation, an engrossing book, a great film, playing tennis or any sport, writing, singing, in times of crisis, when grieving, times of inexplicable joy or whenever we're caught up in the richness of the moment whether painful or pleasurable. Without thought of any unfinished business, even if just for a moment, time seems to stand still. Nothing distracts us. Whatever is going on is all there is. We are present.

One hundred percent immersion is palpable, undeniable and is what this practice is about. Even if we're in the middle of thinking about an important idea or decision, we can train ourselves to disengage from the magnetic pull of the mind when it has nothing to do with the present moment. The value in putting this much attention on mind's relentless nature is simply to become aware of just how relentless and spontaneous it is. It's one of those things that unless experienced has very little meaning.

I happened upon a cure for unwanted thinking in the middle of the night. It was 3:04 a.m. when I looked at my digital clock. Closing my eyes, thoughts of the disturbing film I'd seen the night before grabbed my attention. I followed them for a bit and then wanted to get back to sleep. They continued to engage me with questions. Why do you think . . . .? How did that little girl . . . . ? Half asleep, I consciously focused beyond those queries to a dark space in my mind's eye that was empty of thought— a black hole of sorts. This act made total sense in my sleep state and the next thing I knew, it was morning.

Upon awakening and remembering that interaction, I smiled with satisfaction. I felt I had accomplished something in bypassing the distraction and getting back to sleep so quickly. That space beyond thought, which I knew about intellectually and had played with in the past, had become more deeply and experientially available. Maybe my mind had been more relaxed in this half-awake state. Whatever it was, I'd become one with the empty space beyond the chatter and in that moment all else dissolved. To do that consciously while being barraged with thought felt liberating.

Another night I had a similar experience. This time I wasn't thinking about a film. Instead, I was rehashing a conversation with a client. All the what-ifs were competing for my attention. Again, wanting sleep, I focused on the point beyond thought and again awoke the following morning with that memory.

Presence and Being Complete

During the day, when I remembered to, I would use that technique I happened upon in my dream state. Working on scheduling a workshop, I'd catch myself reliving a conversation I had with a friend the day before. Remembering to switch focus, I'd turn my attention away from yesterday's dialogue to what was in front of me now, all but erasing the distracting thoughts from present time. Vice versa, when the details of my work started to invade my mind while writing an email or talking on the phone, I shifted my attention to what was in front of me, immersing myself fully in that moment. Whether it was an empty space or focusing on what was in front of me to get beyond random thinking, this one-pointed attention was becoming easier to master.

I couldn't control thought, but I could draw my attention away from its gravitational pull. When shifting my attention became difficult, I'd focus on my breath. I noticed sometimes if I was deep in concentration, I'd be holding it or if I were anxious, my breath would become shallow and rapid. To center myself I'd focus on the pause between breaths. If you meditate you're probably aware of this. You simply take a full breath in and then exhale. Before inhaling, you rest your mind on the pause between breaths. In that pause, your mind is still. There is nothing but presence. For that moment your mind is at rest and you're complete. Try it.

Functional thoughts that involve planning activities for home or work—the ones that involve the future — were easy to deal with. To free my mind of the burden of all those details I'd make lists or written plans. Knowing I could find those thoughts again if I wanted to seemed to relax any tendency toward resisting changing focus. Once the list or plan was made, if my mind started thinking about new ideas or something I forgot, I'd simply add to my notes and move on. My mind was all too happy to show me its brilliance at handling distractions. Again, the mind was being a great servant. Given a job, it served well.

Learning a variety of methods to be complete with past and future activities was necessary for me to be at peace. In some ways it was like playing a game. But it was much better to play a game than to come down hard on myself whenever I got distracted.

Relationships — Our Greatest Teachers

The part of this practice that I had the most difficulty with was achieving completion when I was *emotionally attached* to unresolved issues that involved someone who wasn't interested in engaging in resolution, was out of reach or deceased. I understood it intellectually but experiencing it fully, seemed elusive.

In 2009, facing the dissolution of a 10-year friendship gave me the biggest challenge I'd had in years. My friend and I had lived around the corner from each other in Boulder, Colorado before she moved to Maui in 2001. She'd been my touchstone when I first moved on island in 2006 and we equally reveled in once again living so close. Losing her friendship was as near as it comes to losing a sister. Living on Maui felt isolating enough beforehand and without her friendship, I suddenly felt lost.

We went from soul sisters to barely being able to look each other in the eye. Our ease of communication as friends became so polarized that I couldn't even imagine how I'd ever trusted a word she said. In her eyes we were growing apart and in mine issues weren't being dealt with authentically. She felt there was nothing to talk about and I couldn't see how she could walk away from the kind of friendship we had without a shared feeling of completion. I was dumbfounded. But what could I do? Nada!

I was hurt and angry and felt she was insensitive, blind and in denial. My mind was having a field day hashing out all the nuances of our last conversations, looking at all the ways she was amiss and thinking about what I wanted to tell her. But without her cooperation there was no way to reach completion *with* her, so for sanity's sake, I had to reach it with myself. Was life playing with me? This despair came right about the time this practice was introduced. **With the mind racing, it's hard to get any real perspective.**

I went over almost identical conversations in my head countless times until I could barely stand being with myself. I felt like I was back to square one. Writing about my feelings helped a little, but when someone mentioned her name or I ran into her, my anger and hurt surfaced and I realized how obsessed I was. I wanted to stop feeling the way I did. I wanted her out of my head.

During a brief moment of reprieve, I remembered to breathe and focus on the pause after exhaling but couldn't maintain that focus for very long. Then a sanity-saving question arose; *in this moment what do you need to be at peace?* Having something different to focus on, my mind changed direction and the noise stopped. Sound familiar? If you have children, it's the same thing you do when they want something you don't want them to have. You simply distract them with something else of interest. My mind became curious and the light of reason nudged its way in, giving me a breather. Remembering to focus on the breath, my thoughts vacated temporarily and for a few moments I felt complete and at peace.

When the chatter kicked in again like a crowd of people in a shouting match, I'd repeat the question, *what can be done in this moment to be complete?* I'd then breathe deeply and listen for a response that wasn't emotionally charged. Most of the time it was the same, *breathe*. In that moment there really wasn't anything *to do*.

Another time that same question evoked the message, *let go of needing to be right*. Ugh. That was more difficult. I really wanted her to be wrong. I went back and forth on that one—letting go then picking up my righteousness again until pain in my body showed me how holding on to being right was impacting me.

The stress manifested in tightness around my back and shoulders. I'd gone beyond the point of following my thought to its origin, seeing the reality (or non-reality) in that thought and then letting it go. Having taken my dis-ease this far, feeling and then breathing into my pain, a technique I learned from somatic body workers, helped. Like focusing on the breath, it kept me away from incessant thinking. Whatever it took to be complete in the moment and bring peace was my objective. Bringing presence and breath to the pain, my body started letting go.

Besides letting go of being right, the original, subjective thought that triggered me beyond rationale was that she should pay for the hurt I'd felt she caused. Irrational, given all I knew? Most definitely. But just like we don't sit high enough to judge, we don't always know what emotional ghosts haunt us.

Regardless of the culprit, peace was not an option as long as I held on to the thought that she should suffer or that she needed to do any-thing. With the help from a good friend, I saw that I had to forgive myself for reacting and being human and ultimately forgive her for the same. Because this was the final piece of a long process, the act of forgiving felt as if I'd been set free from confinement. That recognition was what finally released me from my internal battle and allowed me to be complete—having nothing to do with engaging her in the process.

Of course, in hindsight it would have been easier to let go and forgive at the onset. But at the time that wasn't what I was capable of doing. If I could have, I would have. Instead, it was a good lesson to glean for future entanglements.

Just like you can't experience how hot water burns the skin by having someone tell you about it, you won't get this practice until you try it. Using all the tools above, breathing, focusing on the pause between breaths, becoming one with physical pain, making lists, getting back to the origin of the thoughts provoking feelings, whatever route works to bring you present and complete in the moment, is the right one for you. In a neutral environment, raging thoughts have nothing to hold on to.

Techniques are obviously not the end-all-be-all but they're useful until shifting focus becomes more automatic or you get to a point where the need to shift, dissipates. The more I engaged in the practice, like a well-worn path, it became easier to find stillness and the moments of being complete increased.

Once the visceral and mental quality of being complete or present in the moment is experienced, like learning how to ride a bicycle, your body's intelligence remembers. To become really good at it, you simply do it over and over again. The mind gives us plenty of fodder to work with. As we get used to feeling a sense of completion in the moment, we learn to deepen and increase the duration of time we spend present and at one with our true nature—the fourth practice.

Key points:

- Take a vacation from the busyness of mind
- Become aware of the subtleties of relentless thinking
- Practice shifting your attention beyond thought
- Focus on your breath to clear your mind
- Being in the present moment is key to being complete
- Being complete in the moment is where peace abides

Inquiries:
- Where is my focus NOW?
- What automatically captures my full attention?
- What can I do to bring myself back to the present moment?
- Am I stressed by over-thinking? How does it show up in my body?
- What does it feel like to be complete in the moment?

Exercise:
Practice being complete in the moment.
1. Observe your mind either in one of your favorite places in nature or during an every day activity. Notice when you're not visually seeing what's right in front of you. Notice the loose ends your mind is attending to. Do what you can to bring completion to those thoughts, following some of the examples in the chapter, and come back to the present moment. Do you need to make a list to let go of details? Do you need to focus on your breath to slow down the internal chatter? Notice that when you are able to be present in the moment, you are naturally complete.

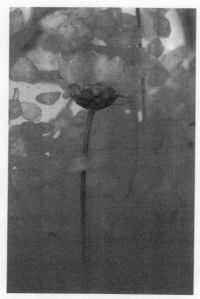

*"Short moments of peace, repeated
many times, becomes automatic."*
~CANDICE O'DENVER

V

PureAwareness

The Fourth Practice

Just like a cat can't do anything more to be a cat and a tree doesn't have to do anything to be a tree, we don't have to do anything to be pure awareness because it's *our* natural, authentic state of being. There's nothing to *do* but *be* what we already are.

The you I'm speaking of is not the personality or the character you have developed nor the roles you've chosen in life. I'm referring to the unchangeable quality of essence that animates your personality, your character and your body.

I'm not sure when I first realized I was more than the sum of my parts (personality, character, body), but when involved with a Hospice organization in Colorado, I heard a chaplain explaining a concept to my client who was dying. She said to the woman, "Think back to when you were little. Is there something within you that still feels the same as when you were that young girl?" The woman thought for a moment and answered, "Yes. It's the part of me I call me." In that moment I turned my consciousness inward to see if I could experience what she was referring to. I instantly knew what she was getting at. It was that same something deep within me that since I was a child I turned to when I felt lost. The chaplain continued and said, "Yes, and that never changes. That is who you are with or without your body."

Her words reminded me of something I heard from Papaji, a disciple of Ramana Maharshi. He said, "Stop looking out there for the truth of who you are. Turn your attention to that which is doing the looking. That's where you'll find what you're searching for, your own true Self." Taking him literally I thought, *could he mean that whatever is looking through my eyes, is what I am?* I discovered that was exactly what he meant. Not the eyeballs, cornea or all its parts, but the awareness looking through.

From that point on, I paid attention to that awareness. I found it was always there. My mind could wander away from it but any time I chose to seek it out, it hadn't budged. When I focused my attention on that awareness, I felt present and connected with a potent force. When my mind drifted, I felt separate from it. But when I'd bring my focus back again, the separation instantaneously disappeared and like a good friend who you can be away from for years, as soon as that connection was renewed, it was like I never left.

And so we come to the fourth practice, *Pure Awareness*. You know how you go on vacation and it sometimes takes a few days, depending on how wound up you are, to actually settle in and relax? I relate to the gradual untangling of the busyness and habits of mind in the same way. The first three practices helped me prepare for the fourth so I could more easily become present and rest in my natural state as pure awareness.

Since pure awareness is who we are when we peel back the layers of identification we've developed around the roles we play, there's really nothing for us to do for this last practice. We simply rest all the trying to fix or figure out *who we are* and instead *be as we are*. We understand there are no problems, we simply do what's obvious and since we know how to be complete in the moment, we're naturally present and at peace.

Throughout the Radiant Mind Training Weekends, we would often just sit in a large room. Not necessarily meditating but just sitting quietly in our chair or on our cushion, eyes open or closed. During those times there was nothing to do, nor understand, and nothing to agree or disagree with. Most of us in the room understood or at least were trying on intellectually, the premise that we were pure awareness and therefore didn't need anything from the training to be our true essence. That established, the context of the weekend and whatever organically happened or didn't happen was in its self, the training.

During these sittings, the room would be very quiet except for the rustling from someone getting up to go to the bathroom or standing to give their rear end or back a rest. If a question arose in someone's mind, they would pose the question to Peter. More than not, the answer to the question would become apparent in the asking. Or the questioner would get what they were doing— allowing the mind to wander into thinking there was really something to get.

At other times the questioner became wrapped up in their inquiry. You could actually see from the expression on their face how intent they were on believing there was something to understand. At that moment, all that was being asked of us was to relax our body and mind while sitting quietly. Taking on the role of a sacrificial lamb, they earnestly quested for truth. As bystanders, the rest of us watched them struggle with the simplicity of being still, seeing the humor in our own over-active minds. When they finally got what they were doing and let go of over-thinking the obvious, they laughed along with the rest of us. Laughing at ourselves saved us all from taking our thoughts so seriously.

Most of us didn't grow up learning the value of doing nothing. Sitting quietly helped us to see how we create something to think about to give ourselves something to do when there is nothing to be done. That incessant need to be busy distracts us from present, pure awareness where if there's really something to do, we'll know it.

Natural Meditation
Even though we don't need to practice being who we are, there are some tools, like just

quietly sitting, that can point us in the direction of seeing that truth. One of the tools I use is a type of meditation called Natural Meditation (NM). It is called NM because it doesn't require any particular skill or method. You can do it as a sitting meditation and a meditation for every waking moment during the normal course of the day.

I usually meditate for about 20 minutes in the morning. I sit with my back straight, either cross-legged or with my feet on the ground out of habit. But unlike other meditations I've worked with in the past, I have nothing to focus on.

Other types of meditations I learned gave instructions to focus on the breath or use a mantra, (specific words that are repeated continuously throughout the meditation) giving the mind something to do to avoid following thought. But sitting NM doesn't require you to stop thinking or quiet the mind. It just requires that you sit still and be with all the thoughts and the possible emotional or physical discomfort, pleasure or any state your thoughts produce and let them be. This doesn't mean you follow and get involved with the thoughts, you simply refrain from expectation, judgment or any need to change whatever's occurring. If silence happens, be with that. If your mind chatters on, be with that. If you have an uncontrollable itch, scratch it. The idea is that eventually, the mind and body will settle down on its own.

Engaging in NM, just like being in a laboratory observing a particle under a microscope, I observed all my tendencies toward needing to move, think about past and future, play reruns of conversations I'd had or might have and reworking ideas or plans. I witnessed my impatience as I checked the time to see if the 20 minutes were up. I noticed how I wanted to be done with what I was doing to get on with what I wanted to do next. All my habits of mind and physical restlessness arose. I had an opportunity to see how I handled being still and how following the stories my mind entertained itself with had become habitual.

The more conscious I became of the trickery of thought, the less I automatically followed it and my time of merely being still, lengthened. At times it felt as if a vacuum cleaner came along sucking all words and feelings out of my field. Nothing but present moment existed. If I tried to force or duplicate that experience, the trying would immediately take me out of the moment. There was nothing to do but be still and alert.

The subtleties of this meditation practice became a template for paying attention during the day. I began noticing when I moved out of the present, grasping for something I wanted or pushing away what I didn't want. I also noticed that every time I allowed life to be as it was without reacting one way or another, I experienced deep peace and whatever I needed or needed to do presented itself even if not the way I thought it would nor in my exact timing.

Blessing in Disguise

In January of 2011 I returned to Maui after spending the holidays with my family at my sister Carolyn's. Shortly after returning I had a severe bout with chills and a 103.5 fever. I figured I had the flu and would get better. When after a few days the fever hadn't normalized, I made an appointment to see the doctor. She took chest x-rays that showed I had pneumonia. With antibiotics, it still took another few days for the fever to go down.

Unable to work or do anything, I'd just lie on my bed or couch. I was highly contagious so friends would come by, announce themselves through the window and place pots of soup on my outdoor table. That was the extent of my interaction with the world.

Most of the time I was even too tired to think. One morning while lying in bed I realized I was more at peace than I could ever remember. With little or no energy, all movement of any kind had ceased. I was simply content to be one with my pillow and mattress. Sometimes, I'd get up and get a drink, heat soup or take care of basic needs. Whatever I did took 100% of my attention.

As I started getting my strength back, I was hyper sensitive to every noise and thought that entered the stillness and was reluctant to give up the spaciousness that had become so familiar. The illness that I now see as a blessing was life changing. I'd been immersed in stillness without any need for being engaged elsewhere. Embodying each moment was all I could do. Naturally slowing down to the rhythm of the moment, I felt full. Although being sick would never be something I'd consciously choose, I wouldn't give up that experience any more than I'd close the door on any great gift.

I was viscerally and psychically imprinted. For those few weeks all my old patterns and beliefs had been suspended or at least so far in the background, they were out of reach. As I starting taking on more daily activity, I felt protective of that spaciousness and was reluctant to fill it up with unnecessary stimuli. Choosing carefully, I eventually got back to a fuller plate with my work and play, grateful for the new appreciation of the presence that sustains us.

Boredom

When relating my peaceful feeling to one of my more dramatically inclined friends, she made a face that was equivalent to sucking on a sour lemon and accompanying her look were equally distasteful sounds. Knowing her well I laughed and said, "Obviously this is not for everyone."

To her the path of peace I'd chosen was extremely boring. And I have to admit that at times the lack of drama in my life is unsettling. Occasionally I miss the intensity of the angst that accompanies wishing life were different. I can feel restless when there is obviously nothing calling my attention and grow antsy from lack of stimulation. That edginess was addicting.

But now when I inquire into my restlessness, I find those feelings of boredom come from thoughts that belong to another place and time. When I'm not distracted by those feelings and instead am okay with feeling what I'm feeling, I remember there is more to the moment and save myself from doing something destructive or exciting just to change my mood.

My first conscious "aha" about boredom came in 2001 during a three-day, solo retreat. I was spending the summer on a 500-acre ranch in Northern New Mexico. The property was owned by an intentional community with which I was affiliated. On my quest I spent three nights and four days tenting along a river on an unfamiliar area of the land. I'd never been on an outdoor solo and chose to do it gently enough to make it somewhat comfortable while sparse enough to gain the benefits of being away from people, stimulation and most modern conveniences.

Like anything new, the first couple of days were filled with wonder. I got used to my surroundings, meditated, wrote in my journal, explored my relationship to life, bathed in the river, danced naked in the early afternoon rain, slept, drank lots of water and ate the dried food and nuts I'd brought along. The second day, besides basking in the natural elements, I also spent time looking at my relationship with fear and my self-incrimination for not being the perfect mother to my sons, Robert and Scott. That night I went to bed at sundown asking the powers that be to show me whatever I still needed to get from these few days.

I awoke with a lot of insights on forgiveness and grabbed my journal so I wouldn't forget anything. Forgiveness was a big part of my reason for choosing this solo and the information helped me see my folly in hanging on and continually blaming myself for what I couldn't change. Basically I saw that I was only holding on because a "good mother," wouldn't let herself off the hook. When that insight really sank in, it made me laugh. Aware of the ludicrousness and insidious ways I caused myself to suffer, I was able to let go.

I put my writing away feeling satisfied. Later that morning after meditating and making tea on my Coleman burner, I felt bored. I sat by the river thinking, *I completed my purpose and made peace with my shortcomings so maybe I should go back*. There didn't seem to be any reason to isolate myself when my friends were back at the main house probably having a great time.

Sitting at the river's edge staring into the water, I noticed sparkles shimmering on its surface from the morning sunlight peeking through the branches of the Sycamore trees. From there my attention turned *to the* birds splashing downstream as they dove and pecked at the water for food. All of a sudden I felt like Alice in Wonderland looking through the keyhole. I was seeing the magic in every little thing. I noticed how the branches that had broken off and fallen in the river created ripples in the bubbling stream as it made its way around or through the stockpile that gathered at the edge of a large bolder. That's when it hit me. Without more dominating stimulation to grab my attention, I was noticing the subtleties I normally overlooked. This was as much a part of my solo as the discoveries around forgiveness. By stopping all the external stimulation, I was privy to an entirely new world.

I sat there for a long time mesmerized by all the more subtle wonders of nature I often overlooked. I took in the colors of the wet logs, the textures of the leaves floating by and the swiftness of the small critters afloat being carried along. I closed my eyes and felt the cool morning air brush my cheek. I was fully present to everything.

I remembered what a trainer in a self-improvement workshop I'd taken in the early 80's said, "If you're bored, you're boring." I hadn't fully gotten the profundity of his words until that moment. If I hadn't stayed and instead packed up and gone back to the house, I would've missed all that exquisiteness and the lesson it provided. Just like beauty is in the eyes of the beholder, so is boredom.

Enjoying the peace-filled pleasures for what they are, I no longer relish the charge from the self-induced drama I used to. If excitement is what I'm looking for, I go to concerts, dance to great music or see an exceptional film, among other alluring entertainment. But since the majority of the time I'm not involved in intense activity, it's been advantageous to cultivate the ability to enjoy the subtleties as well.

Slippery Slope
When gaining awareness of our true nature and engaging with life as pure awareness, we see and feel things with exquisite depth. It's like stepping outside an airport and taking

a breath of fresh tropical air after a long air-plane ride. In this heightened state of aware-ness we feel everything—that which we label as wonderful and everything we label as undesirable. Our senses and feelings take in the entire gamut. We are more fully awake to pain as well as pleasure. Nothing is left behind.

When I get a glimpse or experience that it's all happening just as it should, I see that perfection abides in everything without the notion of good or bad, right or wrong. When I forget, I find myself sliding all over the scale, from numbing myself against what I hear in the news to feeling sadness and anger at those who seem to be destroying all the decency we are capable of. I go between judging life and others from a personal point of view to relaxing judgment and abiding with what is.

Eventually it boils down to this. The less I follow the thoughts that have me see problems where there are simply situations occurring, whether I like them or not, the more the perfec-tion in every moment is revealed. This means trusting that if there is something for me to do, I will be moved in that direction. Now that I look for that validation, I see it happens more than I've realized.

These practices help me see through the stories I conjure up to try and make sense out of the mystery of life. Though interesting at times, my desire for peace outweighs the lure of their attraction. Each moment I'm present and rest as pure awareness, I am at peace.

Key Points
1. "Short moments of awareness, repeated many times becomes automatic."
2. Just like a cat doesn't need to do anything to be more of a cat, you don't have to do anything to be Pure Awareness.
3. Natural Meditation can entrain you to relax and be with everything just as it is.
4. If you're feeling bored, what is present beyond that thought?
5. Blessings can show up in disguise.
6. We don't sit high enough to judge.

Inquiries:
1. Where am I placing my attention?
2. Do my choices bring me peace or stress?
3. If I feel bored, what's beyond that thought?
4. Am I judging or compassionate toward others and myself?

Exercise:

Sit for 20 minutes in Natural Meditation. Feel your feet on the ground; be aware of your breath as you breathe in and out. If you catch yourself following a distracting thought or drifting, notice without judgment and bring your attention back to the present. There's nothing you need to do to be who you already are.

During the day when you can't sit with your eyes closed, notice when you are distracted. Simply bring your attention to present-time. See what is in front of you, and feel your chest rising as you breathe in and out. Become aware of the contact between your feet and your shoes or the ground. As the quote at the beginning of this chapter suggests, *"Short moments of peace, repeated many times, becomes automatic."*

"Take care of your body. It's the only place you have to live."
~JIM ROHN

VI

One More Thing

Iinherited a lot of good things from my mother but along with all that good, came her sweet tooth. Unconsciously, I got in the habit of indulging by treating and consoling myself with sugary snacks whenever I was uncomfortable. And, because I'm weight conscious, where she would have an ice-cream soda, I favored a caffeinated diet coke.

Becoming conscious of my thoughts and how they played with my temperament, I also became aware of how eating excessive sugar and drinking caffeinated beverages made me feel foggy headed and edgy. When I over indulged, I turned into a short-tempered, anxious version of Jasmyne and maintaining focus became extra challenging. The more off-centered I felt, the more I chose unhealthy sustenance for comfort.

My first year on Maui a chiropractic friend introduced me to a nutritional cleanse that included many cleansing nutrients and eliminated all my addictive foods, foods that quickly turn to sugar in the body—i.e., sugar, bread and other simple carbohydrates. It also eliminated caffeine. After the second week of the three-week regime, I noticed a dramatic change in how I felt. My mind was noticeably clearer, I wasn't craving anything and I had more energy. As a bonus, my body as well as my mind became quiet, a most welcome outcome. Eating clean became an ally to the four practices and supported my being present.

Whenever I catch myself feeling "off," it usually has to do with some fear or discomfort. I bring this up because changing perspective about what I put in my body has had a similar affect to my changing perspective with my mind. Just like following distracting thoughts, excessive consumption of sweet treats and caffeine lets me know I'm avoiding the present moment. I don't know if this is true for everyone but it's a practice that works for me.

VII

Epilogue

Writing this book, I learned that you don't write a book so it can be published. You write because you are compelled to do so. And so, I wrote.

As you've probably gathered by now, these practices are guidelines. They're not the end-all-be-all for everyone but simply the practices that were my next step to being at peace and coming home to my true nature.

During the year and a half between the end of the course and the time I started writing **What if the Problem's Not the Problem**, I let go of thinking about the practices but noticed how they'd pop up in my consciousness when I found myself struggling or reacting to life around me. All my human tendencies still played like a ticker tape across my mind. My preferences, judgments and incessant thinking didn't automatically cease after the training. The big difference was that I didn't mistake them for reality. I stopped giving them independent power. If I did get caught in an internal conversation based on fear, the lapse time between my reaction and catching myself was greatly reduced and saved me from a lot of suffering.

To write about how each practice affected my life, I again consciously immersed myself in each one. It was like taking a refresher course. The simplicity and value of each step brought the truth to light once again making as big an impact on me as it had during the course. Whether catching an imagined problem, getting beyond the chatter to listen for a deeper wisdom, finding a way to be complete and in the present moment or knowing there was nothing to do but sit quietly, the support of the practices was invaluable.

Life gives us so many opportunities to live the truth. Each time we take advantage of that fullness and become present, we are that living truth.

To contact Jasmyne about private
coaching or
upcoming writing or transformation classes and
workshops visit:
www.jasmyneconsulting.com

Made in the USA
Charleston, SC
27 February 2013